Bonawit, Stained Glass & Yale

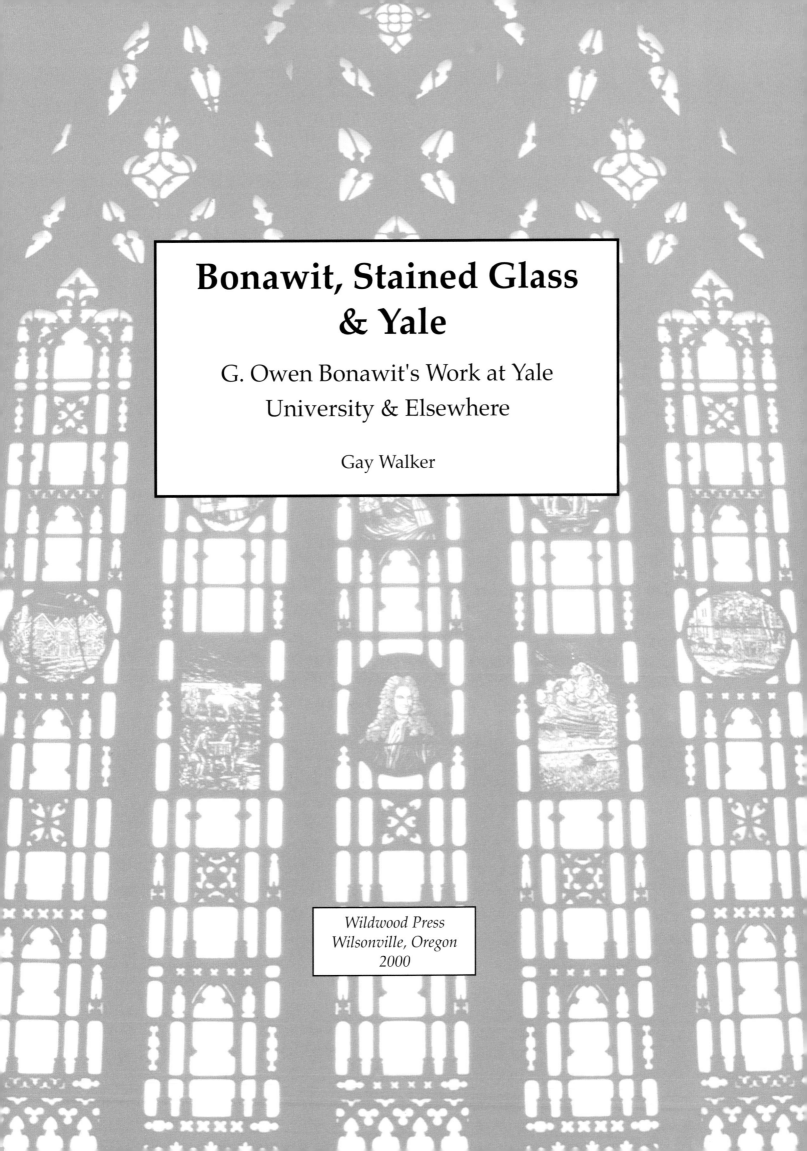

Bonawit, Stained Glass & Yale

G. Owen Bonawit's Work at Yale
University & Elsewhere

Gay Walker

Wildwood Press
Wilsonville, Oregon
2000

This unicorn is one of 46 watermark designs from Medieval
Europe used in the painted medallions decorating the ground
floor work areas of Yale's Sterling Memorial Library.

Half-title illustration: a 16th Century-style bird painted
on a quarry pane in Yale's Sterling Memorial Library, Room 112M.

Title page background image: one of ten large leaded windows in the
entrance hall of Yale's Sterling Memorial Library decorated with
painted panels showing scenes from Yale's history.

©2000 G.Walker, Wilsonville, Oregon
Printed in China

Table of Contents

Above: St Guthlac sailing to Crowland graces a Wall Street window in Yale's Sterling Library. It comes from the 12th Century *Guthlac Roll*, probably the earliest extant model for window medallions.

Overleaf: The Lion and the Mouse from Aesop's *Fables* are the subjects of this medallion in a Special Collections Room (232) in Yale's Sterling Memorial Library.

THE LION AND
THE MOUSE

CHAPTER 1. The Background. Why Gothic?

Yale's Architecture

Most of the glorious stained glass windows at Yale University were crafted by G. Owen Bonawit and his company, a New York firm that worked closely with the Yale Architect, James Gamble Rogers, on many building projects. These projects were designed in the Gothic style and built during the 1920s and 1930s, a time when Frank Lloyd Wright, practitioners of the Bauhaus style, and others were developing new architectural idioms based on functionalism and the clean lines of concrete and glass. Why was the medieval Gothic style chosen for the new Yale buildings? How were the requirements of the educational program at Yale met by this architectural statement? How did stained glass mix with other decorative elements on campus? What was the rationale for selecting the window images? What were those images and how were they made? What other windows relate to those at Yale? This work aims to answer such questions, questions that have often been asked by the denizens of Yale University, those who have attended school, taught, or worked there, and by visitors. Yale's attractive campus focuses on Rogers' Gothic buildings, and their exquisite stained glass windows deserve the considerable attention they attract.

Between 1911 and the mid-1930s, Yale University pursued a major building program beginning with the Harkness Memorial Quadrangle and culminating in the Residential College Plan. The quickly growing enrollment of Yale College and of the graduate and professional schools spurred this unprecedented expansion of housing and teaching facilities that provided eight new undergraduate dormitory colleges, the Law School, the Hall of Graduate Studies, and the central Sterling Memorial Library. Funded privately, these buildings became Yale's architectural and geographical focus, with the University Campus centered around the Library.

Yale had added many buildings between 1870 and 1910 largely designed by the two architects, Cady and Haight, who were well versed in various Gothic building styles. By 1911, Yale's architecture was dominated by a strong Gothic tradition intermixed with many other styles causing one critic to characterize Yale's architecture as "distinguished but inconsistent". No overall plan for the architectural development existed, and there was no real university campus beyond the Old Campus for upperclassmen. Yale properties were scattered among residential buildings, schools, and shops. As plots of land became available, the University would acquire them and build one structure at a time, a practice that discouraged any overall plan or architectural continuity.

Yale University grew tremendously in the 40 years or so extending through the turn of the century, which in turn forced the expansion of Yale's physical facilities. In 1860, the student body numbered 641 with 42 faculty; in 1908 the number of students had jumped to 3,433 with 395 faculty. Until 1911, University officials had advanced no plan for Yale's physical expansion, though an interest in "some degree of architectural unity and impressiveness" had been expressed as early as 1907.

Yale's Building Program

Between 1911 and 1931, Yale received several large gifts that funded the construction of new buildings and spurred the development of an architectural plan for the campus. Major gifts came from the Harkness family in memory of Charles Harkness and from John W. Sterling, all to be spent primarily on buildings. In 1911, the Yale Corporation began the design of a master plan for Yale's expansion by appointing a committee to search for a Consulting Architect who could advise and direct Yale's overall architectural growth. The committee had already decided that it wanted an architect adept in the Collegiate Gothic style, a style defined as:

"strictly American in its origin, it has come to signify that type of domestic Gothic architecture found in the colleges of the Universities of Oxford and Cambridge. These universities are unique among the universities of Europe in their development of the residential college and in their adaptation of a Gothic style to collegiate purposes" (Blackburn, p.11).

The choice of Collegiate Gothic at this point determined the architectural direction for the next 25 years at Yale. Other American universities were also building Gothic structures at this time, notably Princeton, Duke, Bryn Mawr, the University of Chicago, Wellesley, and Northwestern. This academic architectural tradition was associated not only with the seats of English education but with the spirit of the Middle Ages when learning was protected and encouraged within Gothic buildings. The great height, rich decoration, and monumental qualities made Gothic an impressive style thought suitable for a top-rated American university, even though significant architectural developments of the period were being ignored.

The architect chosen for the first building project would be important to the interpretation of architectural style and likely influence subsequent designs for the proposed expansion of Yale. In 1913, James Gamble Rogers, a New York architect and Yale graduate, declined the position of Consulting Architect for Yale. However, he accepted the appointment as Executive Architect for Yale's building program in 1917. His first assignment was to build the Harkness Tower and Memorial Quadrangle, a college dormitory to accommodate 630 students, in the Gothic style.

The Harkness Tower and Memorial Quadrangle, started in 1917 and finished in 1921, established Rogers as a master of the Gothic style. Rogers had traveled through Europe and had studied architecture in France after his Yale education. He drew on this experience for the inspiration and details of these Gothic buildings. Since money was not a limiting factor, the materials were chosen for quality and fitness alone. Rogers' philosophy was that of the master builder in the Middle Ages which encouraged craftsmen to express their individual creativity in the decorative details of the buildings. This approach, coupled with variations in building design, helped Rogers successfully create the "unity in diversity" that was a hallmark of Gothic architecture.

The University next considered plans for physical expansion when Yale received John W. Sterling's bequest of $15 million in 1918, a sum that ultimately produced $39 million for Yale. With the increased enrollment expected following the war, it was apparent that much of the gift would be needed for buildings. In 1919, a new committee was appointed to review all building projects including the proposed Library, the Law

School, and the Hall of Graduate Studies. These three, and particularly the Library, were to become the new focal point of the University. Rogers later commented that "by keeping the modern Gothic well under restraint, the style of the library will not be too much at variance with the architecture of this whole future group, and yet it will express the dignity and importance of the greatest building in the group." Rogers accepted the University's second offer to become Consulting Architect in 1920 and served in that capacity through 1924.

The Sterling Memorial Library

The Sterling Memorial Library was to be a "cathedral of learning," an impressive architectural masterpiece to house the heritage of mankind at a great American university. The Old Library in Dwight Hall was badly overcrowded, and all available storage space in Linsly-Chittenden Hall and other nearby buildings had been exhausted. The architect chosen for the Library was Bertram Grosvenor Goodhue of Boston, who was experienced in the Gothic style. However, in 1924 before construction started, Goodhue died suddenly, and Rogers was asked to take over once more as Executive Architect, a post he held into the mid-1930s. Goodhue's preliminary drawings for the Library were unfinished, so the final design, implementation, and decoration were left up to Rogers. He again turned to the original European Gothic for his inspiration and to the medieval universities of Oxford and Cambridge. The great variety of decorations so typical of the Gothic was carried out in stone, wood, plaster, paint, ironwork, and glass.

A site on two-thirds of the block bordered by Elm, High, Wall, and York streets was chosen for the Sterling Memorial Library. It was a central location half a block from the Harkness Memorial Quadrangle. The site was cleared in 1926, and work began on the massive structure of stone facing a steel skeleton that would bear the weight of several hundred tons of full bookstacks. The building would cost approximately $7 million and was to hold three million volumes with an expansion capacity of five million. The Sterling Memorial Library was officially dedicated and opened in April of 1931.

The Sterling Library was clearly a "cathedral

This scene from *The Poems of Nizami*, edited by Binyon, is based on an illustration by Sultan Muhammad showing Shirin bathing while Khosru looks on (Room 314, Yale's Sterling Library). The two were travelling in opposite directions to wed each other when they met, but this situation was so sensitive that the two did not acknowledge having seen each other and travelled on.

of learning" with its nave, altar, cloisters, crossing, chapels, and side-altars. The Library's entrance and most of the public areas on the ground floor distinctly resembled a Gothic cathedral from the stone floors to the profuse decoration. There were sculpted stone corbels at the junctions of the ceiling arches and carved wooden screens behind the 'altar' of the circulation desk. The ceiling in the entrance nave and the main reading rooms were each 60 feet high, while the clerestory windows soared up from the second story level.

Towards the end of the work on the Library, Rogers designed and built the Sterling Law Buildings and the Hall of Graduate Studies, both in his Modern Gothic style. Each building was characterized by great variety in materials, angles, roof lines, and the profuse detail associated with medieval Gothic architecture.

Stained Glass in America

Stained glass was a traditional aspect of Gothic architecture and provided focal continuity for the extensive decorations in Yale's new building group. Fabricated in the European stained glass tradition of the 12th through the 16th centuries, these Yale windows represented a creative American interpretation of this ancient artistic tradition.

The development of the stained glass craft in America was slow and difficult. Decorative glass manufacturers had been largely unsuccessful into the 19th century, and the majority of decorative and stained glass was imported from Europe, and England in particular. Led by the stained glass revival of the Victorian period in England and the more vigorous influence of the Pre-Raphaelites, America began to produce craftsmen and stained glass for religious settings in the late 1800s. Such windows were made in the traditional medieval style of mosaic (small pieces of glass leaded together) stained glass employing pot-metal colored glass and both painting and staining. The industry was dominated for a considerable period at the turn of the century by the American Art Glass Movement led by John LaFarge and Louis Comfort Tiffany, which was characterized by the use of opalescent glass to produce 'pictures in glass'. A few craftsmen, including Otto Heinigke and his part-

ner, Owen Bowen, continued to produce stained glass in the more traditional manner.

The market for stained glass windows of religious subjects grew substantially after 1900, and American architects began to use local glass and labor. This growth was due in part to the unprecedented numbers of churches and chapels built from 1900 through the 1930s and the popularity of the Gothic architectural style. The American stained glass industry grew to meet the demand and produced craftsmen whose products rivaled European glass. Many men and women became leaders in American religious glass using the medieval cathedral style, among them Henry Wynd Young, Charles J. Connick, Nicola D'Ascenzo, William and Anne Willet, and Henry Lee Willet.

Stained glass images of secular subjects also became popular in America and England during this period, a development with roots in the English, Swiss, and Flemish domestic glass of the 15th and 16th centuries. Secular glass came into vogue for use in commercial, public, and private buildings between 1910 and the mid-1930s. Decorated windows were installed in the homes of wealthy clients as part of an interior decoration plan that might include plaster friezes, painted murals, and glazed tiles. These window decorations featured mosaic leaded glass, decorative leading, and painting on glass panels. Somewhat closer to the scenic pictures of the Art Glass craftsmen, this secular glass movement used the methods and materials of the medieval glass craft but achieved a better balance between decoration and the admission of daylight. Among those working in this genre, G. Owen Bonawit was one of the foremost, specializing in the delicate painting of secular subjects on clear glass panels.

James Gamble Rogers selected Bonawit and his firm, G. Owen Bonawit, Inc., of New York City, to provide the several thousand window decorations for Yale's Sterling Memorial Library, the Hall of Graduate Studies, and many of the residential colleges. The windows in the Library constituted an extraordinary group of secular glass decorations in both quality and quantity. Fabricated in a period immediately preceding a great decline in the craft, Bonawit's painted windows were among the best of a creative American development.

Upper left: "Omar under the Bough" by Edmund Dulac from the 1919 Fitzgerald edition of Omar Khayyam's *Rubaiyat* was the source for the painted panel (**upper right**) in Room 107M of Yale's Sterling Library. **Lower left:** This medallion in Room 329, home of the American Oriental Society Library, shows a scene from the *Book of the Dead*, Papyrus of Anhai (**lower right**). Isis and Nephthys, sisters of Osiris, kneel on either side of the standard of the West which supports the hawk, or Ra-Harmacbis.

CHAPTER 2. The Sterling Memorial Library Window Decorations

The soaring arched window full of tracery, richly decorated and brilliantly colored, typified the spirit of Gothic architecture. For Yale's Sterling Memorial Library, Rogers designed tall mullioned windows with intricate tracery and filled them with leaded quarries and painted decorations following the medieval tradition. The decorations for the Library windows were designed to illustrate the purpose of the building as well as to provide variety and detail. Rogers described the planned Library decorations in 1928.

"The Ornamentation is studied to symbolize the great or interesting facts connected with libraries, bibliography, books, etc., and not the history of Yale. The latter has been adequately covered in the Memorial Quadrangle, which is a fitting place for the memorials of the deeds of Yale men. A library has a broader field. As a general scheme the main or entrance hall will contain in its decoration the history of the Yale Library, but the decoration in other places will symbolize the history and universality of the libraries of the world" (Rogers, "The Sterling Memorial Library," p.7).

The window decorations constituted the greatest number of designs in any medium in the building and formed a coherent group of decorations that delineated not only the "universality of the libraries of the world" but the entire world of learning.

The variety of decorations in other media found in the Library, notably the stone sculptures, wood carvings, ironwork, and decorative painting and plastering, was matched in the windows by the variety in form, color, style, and subjects of the designs. The painted clear glass panels, or medallions, so widely used were of various shapes: rectangular, square, circular, oval, and uneven-sided. These panels were set in leaded windows and surrounded by smaller quarries in rectangular or diamond patterns. The quarries, small panes with parallel sides, were used in Medieval decorated glass as background or borders to larger designs. They often became the entire decoration in the 15th and 16th centuries. Bonawit decorated them with patterns or small figures and scattered them over the windows. Another form of decoration was the mosaic stained glass in the many

heraldic shields, the only pot-metal colored glass in the Library. The delicately painted surrounding quarries in these and other windows provided an appealing contrast to the bright colors of the pot-metal glass. The eclectic styles and subjects of the original images used for most of the window designs also provided great variety although the decorations were unified by a continuity in the painting style. The artist paid great attention to the arrangement of each design, the relation of clear glass and leading to the painting, and the careful draughtsmanship of the painting itself.

Consistent with the philosophy of the medieval master builder, Rogers gave Bonawit a wide latitude in the final fabrication of the designs and total freedom in creating the many images not based on supplied illustrations. Although Bonawit and his staff also 'designed' these decorations, the majority of the images closely followed the printed illustrations provided to the firm. Like other stained glass studios, Bonawit's had a staff that included designers as well as glass cutters and kilnsmen, and it is difficult to distinguish individual work, but Bonawit was ultimately responsible for the overall style and quality of output.

Bonawit's firm fabricated approximately 3,300 stained glass decorations along with decorative leading and other non-window glass decorations and installed them in the Library in just over a year. This amazing output was even more impressive given that several other Yale buildings with large numbers of glass decorations by Bonawit were being built at roughly the same time, and that the firm also provided decorative glass to contractors outside of Yale.

The window decorations crafted for the Sterling Library were particularly well-suited to the Gothic architecture of a library. The artist faced several problems in fabricating the designs: the majority of the window decorations were to be intimately viewed at eye-level rather than from a distance; the decorations were for a library and not a cathedral, though the structure was cathedral-like; and most of the designs were to be based on sources totally eclectic in both style and subject matter while others were to be designed free-hand. All decorated glass was to be installed in a new building in a short time-frame. Bonawit happily resolved these problems, and this project showed his particular flare for creating designs appropriate to their settings.

Medieval glass craftsmen employed several methods of glass painting for detailed work according to the location of the window. The detail on a window placed at eye-level, for instance, would usually be finer than that on a window placed at a distance above the viewer, or a small image might have more detail than a large one. The most popular technique, called "stick-work", involved applying a wash, drying it, and then scratching out the highlights, details, or shading with a stick or stiff brush. The opacity and shade of color depended on the thickness of the coating applied. By this means, very fine detail was possible. Cross hatching and stippling were also used to build up the background or shading. In virtually every painted window, Bonawit used the wash/scratch technique. Many window designs in the 60-foot high Entrance Hall and the five major public rooms on the ground floor were placed far above the viewer, but these designs were as detailed as the others. An exception is the central window over the entrance. It comes closest to displaying the full decoration of cathedral windows. This window lacks fine details and, instead, is filled with larger-than-life figures made of brass covered in lead with almost no painting or color beyond the features and a stain for the hair. The details of these figures are both stylized and highly decorative, lending them an Art Deco flavor.

Although the Sterling Library was so obviously designed after a Gothic cathedral with its vaulted ceilings, tall mullioned and traceried windows, cloisters, and courtyards, it was a library. This difference posed a particular problem for the designer of the window decorations. A library needs more light than a cathedral, and the rich full-color stained glass that obscures the natural light in medieval cathedrals would be inappropriate in a Reading Room, for instance. The architect realized this problem and planned for the maximum number of windows, probably for the sake of symmetry as well as increased lighting. As an illustration, the Main Reading Room has tall windows on the northern wall that admit considerable light from a very narrow space left between this room and the body of the Library, even though the room could more economically have shared a wall.

Several forms of secular glass decoration produced by the Bonawit firm were extremely suitable to this setting, most notably the painted and stained panel of 12" x 18" or smaller, and the painted quarry. While most of the smaller windows placed at eye-level in the studies and seminar rooms were decorated with one painted panel and sometimes as many as four in the larger windows, the monumental windows in the ground floor public areas were decorated with strong leaded designs and many painted glass panels so the decorations would not be lost in the larger expanses of clear glass panes. For example, the ten windows in the Entrance Hall each contained eight painted panels placed midway in the frame. In the original Periodical Reading Room, each of the six windows was decorated with six painted and stained panels surrounded by the signs of the zodiac in leading. This provided enough decoration to balance the setting but not limit the light. Thus, Bonawit provided full window decorations but not at the expense of the light necessary for the purpose of the building.

Even the full-color heraldic shields in the Main Reading Room windows provided decoration only at the top of the windows with the exception of the two large bay windows, each with 22 shields. These decorations created shafts of color mellowed by the strong natural light surrounding them. The other decorations in these windows were small painted figures and patterns in outline, taken from 15th century designs (see Day, *Windows*, p.282-3) and numbering around 1,630. They are scattered over the windows in delicate contrast to the brightly-colored and boldly leaded shields. Bonawit added small figures to the quarries in many other rooms as well, providing ornamentation but not blocking the light.

Bonawit also met the challenge of working with widely varying subjects and sources in many styles. The majority of the designs were provided to the artist in the form of book illustrations taken from library holdings. For the most part, the illustrations were closely followed though artistic license was taken in various alterations, particularly in the background and, at times, the layout of the subject to fit the space available. The sources were eclectic and ranged from photographs to sketches to printed plates in a wide variety of compositions and artistic styles. The challenge was to create a sense of coherence in all the window decorations while maintaining the variety and individual liveliness of the original compositions. Bonawit achieved this by controlling the placement and composition of the designs and by crafting all the designs using the same painting techniques. The individual flavor of the original source is retained and the style is still recognizable, but the overall treatment shows a definite continuity. The painted panels are characterized by the dark brown outlines, the stick-work on a base of brown wash, and the prevalence of staining as the only color.

Those designs left up to the imagination of the artist represented the personal style of Bonawit and his firm, often showing a distinct influence of the Art Deco style of the 1920s and 1930s. Many elements of these designs were highly stylized, and though most of the figures were fairly relaxed, they were also stylized and verged on becoming decorative patterns. In this sense, Bonawit was following the philosophy of the traditional stained glass movement in America which started just before the turn of the century. Otto Heinigke, one of its leaders, felt that "the human figure when used in decoration must be translated into ornament, governed by the style of the building it is to decorate". A book illustrator working in the same Art Deco style was Rockwell Kent, with whom Bonawit had been compared, although Bonawit consistently employed more decorative details. The figures in the large window over the entrance showed this influence, but the largest group of Art Deco window designs was found in the original Periodical Reading Room. This style was particularly appropriate for Rogers' Modern Gothic architecture and related well to the stone relief work on several of Rogers' nearby buildings, including the Hall of Graduate Studies and Trumbull College next door to the Library, in which the flat surface is incised without further relief carving. Bonawit's own artistic style thus enhanced the overall variety and richness of the Library's window decorations.

CHAPTER 3. The Window Designs: Selection, Sources, and Treatment

Selection

The Library staff and members of the Yale community participated in the choice of subjects for the Sterling Library decorations that were to symbolize the world of learning. The window designs would represent the purpose of each room by showing significant images for every field of learning.

In January of 1928, two years after library construction began, a Committee on Decoration for the Library was appointed comprising the Head Librarian, Andrew Keogh; the Dean of the Art School; the Dean of Branford College; the President ex officio; the Secretary of the University; and the architect's representative. Mary Withington, Mr. Keogh's private secretary, maintained the minutes and correspondence of this Committee and played a major role in locating the design subjects.

The Committee on Decoration began to submit design subjects for the window decorations early in 1930, about a year before completion of the Library building. The Committee's subject lists for the window decorations were drawn up over a six-month period ending in June of 1930. The Committee chose the window designs last, after the stonework and other media, due to the sequence of construction stages.

Meeting periodically in the Librarian's Office, the Committee on Decoration suggested and reviewed subjects for the window designs. Miss Withington compiled a list of proposed subjects after each meeting to send to the members for final approval, whereupon she and other staff members tracked down books and other sources that supplied many of the illustrations used as window designs. The illustrations were sent off to be photographed by a local firm and printed as photostats. The positive photostats were given to Bonawit's firm to be used as working guidelines which were then destroyed. The Library staff collected either a second positive or the negative photostat of most of the designs into a two-volume scrapbook now deposited in the Library Archives, although no records exist for a large number of the designs.

Although the Committee on Decoration sug-

Dante Gabriel Rossetti illustrated his poem, *The Blessed Damozel*, with this image, which shows the maiden looking down from heaven at the souls mounting up to God and at her lover. The poem first appeared in 1850. The image as shown in Yale's window (Sterling Memorial Library, Room 215, originally the English Study) leaves out several heads in order to simplify the design.

gested the subjects for each study room in the Sterling Library tower and the overall ideas for the public areas, the actual designs were chosen in several ways. Miss Withington and the Library staff found the illustrations for most of the subjects and sent them to Bonawit. General suggestions for several of the rooms were handed to Bonawit with the designs left to his selection and artistry, and outside experts and faculty were consulted in a few subject areas. In some cases, whether the sources were located by the library staff or by the artist, or whether the designs were freely created by Bonawit is a matter of conjecture.

The Committee reviewed design subjects for an entire discipline at a time, and each subject list covered the rooms associated with one field of knowledge. In at least one case, the list included general suggestions of literary and historical scenes or personages with recommendations for sources of descriptions rather than of book titles or illustrations. The Committee members chose subjects they felt represented the most important historical figures, events, or writings for each discipline, an interesting view of what was perceived as important at the time. All illustrations submitted to Bonawit were from printed books, manuscripts, or other holdings of the library in 1930. The subject lists were gathered into a checklist, added to the much smaller list of decorations in other media, and published in the special decoration issue of the *Yale University Library Gazette* in April of 1931.

Many subjects on the Committee lists were annotated with the phrase, "No Picture." Although no photostats were sent to the artist, many can be identified in books. The artist no doubt located the appropriate sources himself as he did in at least one other major commission for some of the windows in the Deering Library of Northwestern University, or he may have selected illustrations from general volumes provided by the library staff. In many instances, the artist created new designs, as in the original Periodical Reading Room with its 36 allegorical figures representing Time. In the Entrance Hall, only the descriptions were provided for 23 of the 80 designs showing the history of the Yale Library. Along Wall Street on the ground floor, window decorations were described only as showing "episodes from mediaeval life, and knights from

manuscripts and monk drawings of the time." Other decorations, such as those in the central window over the Main Entrance, all the heraldic shields, and the designs in Room 509 and elsewhere, were also designed entirely by Bonawit.

It is clear that Bonawit had latitude in the fabrication of the window designs and a free hand in some, although the Committee on Decoration closely scrutinized all the *subjects* for the Library decorations, and the majority of the sources came from Library holdings. A few of the decorations were closely related to designs used by Bonawit in earlier commissions for which he "scoured American paleontology and archaeology for subjects." One example is the pair of frogs found in Room 335 of the Sterling Library and in the earlier Cunard Building windows fabricated in 1921.

Sources

The library staff and the artist consulted a great number and variety of sources for the window designs. Some sources provided more than one design, though usually no more than ten. A few volumes were more heavily used as design sources, the two most notable being Charles Briquet's *Les Filigranes*, a four-volume compendium of early watermarks published in 1923 from which 46 designs were taken for windows in the ground floor work areas, and the famous book of Jost Amman, *Stände und Handwerker*, a volume of woodcuts depicting occupations originally published in 1568. This volume supplied 99 illustrations, several being used more than once. However, the great majority of the 679 designs were located individually, one illustration from each book. An enormous amount of time and research effort were invested in locating the sources, whether found by the library staff or the artist.

A great variety of illustrators and illustrations were used as design sources. Only a few illustrators were represented more than once, such as Jost Amman. Nine designs were taken from the Gutenberg *Bible*, 28 from Walter de Milemete's manuscript treatise in the *Dialogus Creaturarum* (written in 1483), and four from Hans Burgkmair's woodcuts in his 1775 *Weiss Kunig*, which describes the life of Kaiser Maximilian I. Of the more modern illustrators,

Upper right: This painted and stained bird, based on a German naturalist work, graces a window in Room 335 (originally a Special Collection) in Yale's Sterling Library. The close-up (**upper left**) shows the careful use of wash and the fine stickwork detail. **Lower left:** A male Japanese dancer/actor of the 18th Century decorates a window in Room 333, originally the Far Eastern Collection. **Lower right:** An image from the manuscript, *Speculum Humanae Salvationis* , is in Room 212, originally a Special Collection. Note the lead lines that run across unimportant parts to give an antique appearance.

Edward Corbould and Grandville, both popular late 19th century artists, were represented several times. All seven of the designs in the original James Fennimore Cooper Collection, Room 218, were based on Felix O.C. Darley's illustrated edition of Cooper's works, and Darley's illustrations provided the designs for *Rip Van Winkle*, *The Legend of Sleepy Hollow*, and *Reveries of a Bachelor* in Room 219. Contemporary artists' works were also chosen, including works of Arthur Rackham, Jessie Willcox Smith, and Edmund Dulac. One group of designs in particular had a special relevance to the stained glass tradition. Four of the images in the Wall Street ground-floor windows were taken from the *Guthlac Roll*. The *Roll* was a late 12th century work containing 18 pictures drawn in ink that illustrated the life of St. Guthlac of Lincolnshire, England. It is generally believed that these medieval medallions, six inches in diameter, were the earliest surviving design sketches for stained glass windows. Though no such windows survive, various authorities believe that the simple composition, monochrome colors, and unusual size of these drawings support the window design theory.

Design sources drew on more than artists' illustrations. The 10 designs in the Babylonian Collection rooms show the ceramic murals of ancient Assyrian cities from Layard's *Monuments of Ninevah*. The design for the portrait of Elihu Yale in the Entrance Hall was copied from his personal snuff box held at Yale, while another Entrance Hall window design was based on an illustration from a student playbill. Both ancient and modern illustrations in many media were used from the entire range of sources: printed books; facsimile publications; sales catalogs; manuscripts; bookplates; and objects. The designs were eclectic and truly representative of the broad spectrum of the world of learning from the history of the Yale Library itself, of the University, and of New Haven, to the history of universities in general, of printing, and of every major area of study.

Treatment

Bonawit altered many of the illustrations given him as sources for the window designs for technical or aesthetic reasons. On another stained glass commission, he was explicit about the necessity for the artist to interpret sources into creative designs, and he felt that "you cannot copy a medieval window, but you can be inspired by one." He went on to discuss the suitability of the window decorations to the setting:

> If we had been assigned modern subjects for the windows, we should not have used medieval design but should have designed the windows in a modern manner. If medieval subjects had been assigned, such, for example, as historical episodes of the twelfth and thirteenth centuries, we should have designed in that period. If necessary, we could design medieval subjects in modern drawing, but in doing this we should lose the sincerity and greatness of medieval art" (Blackburn, p.27).

Bonawit followed the individual style of each illustration but he used the same painting techniques throughout to give continuity, and he controlled the choice and placement of elements in the design, the amount of clear glass remaining, and the treatment of details through omission, addition, and alteration. These changes enhanced the design by simplifying it or by increasing the interest of the composition.

The changes made by the Bonawit firm between illustration and painted design may be illustrated by several examples. For instance, Bonawit focused on the foreground figures from the illustration in Mark Twain's *Innocents Abroad* in Room 219. The elimination of the complicated background helped avoid confusion in the glass panel. Changing the amount of clear space around the central image in Arthur Rackham's illustration of the ass in the lion's skin from Aesop's *Fables* in Room 232 both emphasized the figures and lightened the scene, creating a better balance between the panel and the surrounding clear glass quarries. By simplifying the design of the cook, a Maxfield Parrish illustration for the cover of *Harper's Weekly* in Room 107M, Bonawit was able to concentrate the viewer's attention on the figure. The magazine cover showed scenery out the window behind the cook which Bonawit eliminated, since the Library view would provide new scenery. Leaded windows were added in two compositions in which the original illustrations had no background: one is the Jack Spratt and his Wife design in Room 107M. It is amusing to note that some of the painted quarries in this design are mended and stained.

Upper left: The cook in Yale's Library's Room 107M is based on Maxfield Parrish's cover illustration (**lower left**) for *Harper's Weekly*, December 14th, 1895. The close-up (**upper right**) demonstrates the effective use of wash to give dimensionality to the picture. **Lower right:** The heraldic shields in the Sterling Library in the Main Reading Room, along Wall Street, and in Room 112M (shown here) demonstrate the mosaic style of glass fabrication with a wash patina to simulate weathering. Note also the small designs based on 16th Century European domestic glass (as shown in Day's *Windows* of 1909).

Bonawit and his artists made more basic alterations on a number of illustrations in their transfer to the painted panel. One of the angels and the upper part of the scene were omitted in "The Blessed Damozel" composition by Rossetti in Room 215, changes that simplified the design. In another window in Room 215, Alice was moved to stand in front of the Duchess in Tenniel's illustration for *Alice in Wonderland*, a change that allowed both figures to fit comfortably in the panel. All these variations helped focus the viewer's attention on the central subject and to improve the clarity and composition of each. In the great majority of cases, however, Bonawit and his artists followed the original illustration with great success, either filling the panel with the scene or leaving the picture in its original shape with clear glass around it.

Even though these painted window decorations were translucent pictures on glass, a much-criticized format by some who preferred the more traditional mosaic pot-metal stained glass windows, the images were uniquely suited for secular window decorations. The use of the dark outline drawings and the simple staining technique did not obscure the natural light but drew attention to the window surface as a two-dimensional plane, often distracting the viewer from an uninteresting background. As with all window decorations, Bonawit's painted panels were affected by the quality and intensity of light behind them, particularly in judging the shade of the stain. However, since the panels did not modulate the daylight to any noticeable extent, interiors never appeared gloomy or too dark because of them. Even in the windows decorated with full-color heraldic shields, the designs comprise such a small part of the window that, while they commanded attention and provided an accent of bright color, the design did not affect the overall amount of the transmitted light.

CHAPTER 4. Production of Glass Decorations

The Bonawit firm used Medieval stained glass techniques in a craft that had changed little since Medieval times except in the ease of obtaining supplies, the control of coloring the glass, and the type of kiln. Much of the colored glass for Bonawit's work came from England, France, and Belgium from manufacturers proficient in the ancient trade of glass making.

Medieval Stained Glass

The European stained glass industry flourished from the 12th through the early 15th centuries, declined in the late 15th and 16th centuries, and enjoyed a revival in the Victorian period. Stained glass developed concurrently with Gothic architecture and was an important architectural element, giving color and beauty to the tall arched windows that told stories to the worshippers. Builders filled their cathedrals with stained glass windows, usually placed at a distance from the viewer, which severely restricted the entry of natural light. Early medieval glaziers formed the windows from many small pieces of colored glass held in place with long pieces of H-shaped leading, or cames. The glass painter added a few strokes or slight shading here and there in a dark brown color to indicate the features, drapery, or other details and used a yellow stain as the only other applied color. This method produced the "mosaic" stained glass so typical of the period, and it was the only technique of stained glass fabrication until the late 14th and early 15th centuries.

As artists sought a more naturalistic representation of the actual world in the 14th and 15th centuries, glass craftsmen also shifted away from pure colored glass pieces leaded together. The glass painter became more important until painting dominated the work of the glazier, realism being less easily achieved in mosaic stained glass. The painter became master of the craft, even to the point of ignoring leading altogether in the 16th century and later. This move towards the pictorial in making "pictures on glass" along with the influence of the Renaissance and the trend away from Gothic architecture caused a sharp decline in the production and quality of stained glass until the Gothic Revival in the 19th century.

Secular stained glass decorations for domestic use became popular in the 15th and 16th centuries in the Flemish, Swiss, and English glass tradition. Secular glass portrayed heraldic or pictorial subjects incorporating portraits and historic or domestic scenes for both public and private buildings. Flemish craftsmen made extensive use of the smaller painted panel showing figures or scenes surrounded by a painted and leaded border. The leading acted as a frame for the picture and emphasized the pictorial while more light was transmitted by using clear glass and translucent colors.

In England, Queen Elizabeth decreed that glass was to be plain and that all glass-paintings of a superstitious nature were to be destroyed. Heraldry thus became the popular subject for English window decorations in the mid-16th and 17th centuries. Families had their coats of arms, usually done in the mosaic stained glass method, placed into leaded windows in their great country houses and castles. The art of etching flashed glass, clear glass coated with a colored layer, was particularly widespread so that details could be added to the shields, while the decorative use of painted quarries was universal in both England and on the Continent at this time.

The tradition of medieval religious stained glass, then, was originally the art of designing and glazing pot-metal colored glass pieces with some painting on them in the mosaic method for use in Gothic cathedrals. The secular tradition of stained glass developed during the later phases of the art to fill a decorative need on the personal level as the general populace became more affluent. Although craftsmen produced secular glass decorations with the techniques used for religious glass, the product was totally different; secular work emphasized the pictorial with leading used as a frame rather than as a structural part of the central design.

Fabrication

The fabrication of a traditional mosaic stained glass window usually started with a sketch. The sketch was made into a full-scale colored or color-coded paper drawing that was cut into the various shapes allowing for an 1/8" leading strip between pieces. The artisan followed the paper guides in cutting out the colored glass pieces. Once cut, the pieces were attached to a clear glass plate with a light source behind it using beeswax or some other fixative. Then the painter outlined the features, draperies, and other details using vitreous dark brown glass paint and wash if desired. Various painting techniques were used to introduce highlights or background and shading. The stain was applied to the backside of the glass, on what would be the outside of the window. The pieces were fired to the melting temperature of the glass paint and of the glass surface to insure permanent adherence. At this point, if both the stain and paint had been properly applied and fired, they became fixed and impervious to scraping or weathering. After firing, the pieces of glass were placed in order and joined by the H-shaped lead cames, the two flanges fitting around the pieces of glass and holding them in place. All joins were soldered on both sides. A cementing wash was brushed on last to fill in the cracks between the leading and the glass, and the lead flanges were pressed down. This made the window waterproof and darkened the cames. The window was then ready for installation. The painted panels used in late Medieval windows differed only in that each was painted, stained, and fired as a single piece before being leaded into the window.

Production of the Sterling Library Window Decorations

The fabrication of the majority of the Sterling Library window decorations was particularly close to the late medieval practice of painting scenes on clear glass panels set in leaded windows, while the colored heraldic shields and the leaded windows surrounding the painted glass panels were done in the more traditional mosaic manner. Most of the illustrations were submitted to the artist in their original size, one as small as 2" x 3". Only two of the 679 painted panels in the Library were repeated, an image from the *Sphaera mundi* (1488) of Sacro Bosco in both the Exhibition Corridor and Room 609, and a Persian miniature from the *Diwan* of Auhadi of Kirman in the Entrance Hall and Room 314. The Bonawit firm would have cut each clear glass panel to the proper size, painted the design using a dark wash, a deep brown vitrifiable paint for the outlines, and various Medieval painting techniques, applied the stain on the back side, and then fired the panel to bond the paint and stain to the glass. The panel would then be leaded into the larger window and

Over: The full-color painted glass panel showing David fighting Goliath is taken from a 15th Century French *Breviary*, or *Book of Hours*, an illuminated manuscript held by the Yale Art Gallery. This close-up of Goliath shows both the wash technique and the fine stickwork of the glass artists. The window, at eye-level, is in the entrance hall of Yale's Sterling Memorial Library near the public computers.

installed in the sash or casement in the Library.

The colorful heraldic shields, which form the upper window decorations along Wall Street and in the Main Reading Room, were made in the traditional Medieval mosaic method using a minimum of painting and a patina wash to give an ancient appearance. The shields do not represent actual coats-of-arms but were created as colored patterns using heraldic conventions of quartering and geometrical designs. Although no etched glass has been identified in the Library, the Bonawit firm did use this method in other Yale work, such as for the shields in the Hall of Graduate Studies where the etched areas were either stained or left clear.

Leading was needed to hold the small glass pieces together in the large Gothic windows. All the Sterling Library windows were leaded, or glazed, following the Medieval tradition. The early European glass industry produced fairly small pieces of glass, usually from glass blown into cylinders that were then slit open into flat sheets. Less common techniques included twirling glass into sheets and rolling out flat sheets. Often very small pieces of glass were leaded together, and many thousands of pieces might have gone into a large window. The H-shaped lead cames were quite soft and could be cut and bent around any glass shape. The standard Library windows consisted of small diamond shaped and rectangular quarries, the usual size being 6" x 8". Clear, cloudy, and light pastel shades of quarries were used irregularly, a traditional Medieval practice.

The Bonawit firm produced all the painted and stained decorations while the Henderson Brothers, another New York firm, produced the bulk of the typical undecorated leaded windows, working closely with Bonawit on several of these commissions. The Bonawit firm installed all the glass on the ground floor and produced all the painted medallions for the upper floors, delivering 473 of them to the Henderson Brothers' shop in New York, who then inserted the medallions into the leaded windows before installation.

Staining was a method of coloring glass discovered in the early 14th century when, according to one legend, a glassman's silver cuff button caught on a piece of glass as it went into the kiln and produced the stain. The stain was normally obtained by applying silver oxide or silver chloride to the back of the glass. When fired, a chemical change took place in the glass and a permanent yellow color resulted. Depending on the strength of stain applied and the level of heat, the color could range from a pale lemon yellow to a deep rich orange or gold. In many of the late Medieval glass decorations, staining was the only coloration, particularly in the painted quarries, and was widely used for hair, beards, and crowns in mosaic stained glass. Bonawit used stain alone for the coloring of all but six of the painted glass panels in the Sterling Library windows. He used stains with such mastery that the yellows, oranges, and golds combined with the brown outline paint and wash often made the window decorations appear to be full-color designs.

The brown outline paint had been used since the earliest period of stained glass in the 12th and 13th centuries. The painting was done with a very dark brown, almost black, color of vitreous glass paint made of ground glass, a metal oxide (oxide of iron or manganese), and a liquifier such as water or oil to give the proper consistency for painting. The liquid burned off during firing. A flux was also added which lowered the melting point of the paint just enough so that only the surface of the painted glass would melt to bond permanently with the paint. The paint was applied with a brush in strokes or as a matte wash. The design or shading was then scratched out of the dried wash with a stick or stiff brush to produce complex background patterns and highlights as well as various shades of color. Other Medieval methods of painting included cross-hatching and stippling to give shading and patterns. The Bonawit firm employed the brown outline paint, the wash, and the stick-work technique in almost every painted panel in the Library, all showing extremely fine detail. The very few exceptions without stick-work are more "painterly" but are not as successful, although perhaps more fitting to the subject.

Several colors of vitrifiable paint were used to produce full color small glass pictures without leading in six of the windows in the ground floor Entrance Hall looking into the Librarian's Courtyard. The paints were made with different metallic oxides but had the same properties as the brown outline glass paint. The colors were bright and were set off nicely by the decorative leading surrounding them. The pictures were extremely complex and detailed and added a rich touch to this area.

Quarries, both decorated and clear, were common to all periods of Gothic stained glass from the 12th century on, and they were used throughout the Sterling Library. The subjects of the painted quarries found in several areas in the Library were exact replicas of 15th century designs and were used in the same decorative tradition. These designs were scattered over the windows forming a two-dimensional pattern that could distract from an unattractive view but still admit light easily.

Other styles of quarry painting based on Medieval practices were also used. Delicate paintings decorated the administrative offices including a life-sized dragonfly and bee, perhaps meant to fool the viewer as a *trompe l'oeil* image, similar to the practice in Medieval Flemish domestic glass. Several of the quarries in the leaded windows of Room 333 showed painted Japanese sword guards, a complement to the panels in the same windows of Japanese dancers, warriors, and ladies. Together, these decorations served to hide the view of a parapet two feet beyond the window that rises up to half the windows' height. The neighboring room with the same obstructed view contained windows covered in painted pictures that flowed across the leaded quarries, particularly appropriate for the animal forms chosen to represent the purpose of the room, a natural history study. The marine animals at the bottom of the window and the birds in flight higher up against a blue sky gave a wonderful effect.

Rogers added several humorous touches to his Modern Gothic style based on Gothic cathedrals in the 20th century, and Bonawit followed suit in the window decorations. For instance, Rogers left several stone niches empty in the Library and elsewhere at Yale (e.g., the Harkness Tower) to resemble the sacked cathedrals of Europe. The elevator machinery on the Library's roof, called the "Pent House," was encased in decorated steel sheathing looking much like a Medieval French pavilion with its turrets and metal banners. Bonawit deliberately made glass look old in imitation of Gothic win-dows aged by centuries of time and weather. Many of the clear glass quarries had "mending" leads across them where cracks were planned. Every panel in the set of painted Medieval deco-rations in Room 212 looked like it had been bro-ken and then mended, the lead cames conve-niently crossing the least important areas of the design and never covering a figure's face. A light patina wash was used on some painted panels and on the heraldic shields to give them a slightly muddy, aged quality.

In summary, the decorative glass produced by the G. Owen Bonawit firm was closely related in technique and materials to the Medieval tradi-tion but was crafted with a fresh interpretation, called by one critic a "peculiarly native use of stained glass." Although some critics felt that transparent glass pictures represented the decline of the stained glass art at the end of the Middle Ages, this method was used to great advantage by Bonawit. The designs were not simply transparent glass pictures but were well-planned decorations that interacted with the leading design in the window, with the other panels in nearby windows, and with the archi-tecture of the room itself. In many cases, they presented a two-dimensional decoration designed to obscure an unattractive view. The painting was handled with great confidence and creativity, and the subjects were lively and emi-nently suited to their setting. The window deco-rations provided continuous variety and a delightful reminder of the world of learning sur-rounding the library patron.

CHAPTER 5. G. Owen Bonawit

The G. Owen Bonawit firm produced the immense number and variety of glass decora-tions for the Sterling Memorial Library in just over a year, February of 1930 through April of 1931, while simultaneously providing decorative glass for several other commissions. Roger's long-standing relationship with Bonawit result-ed in huge quantities of decorated glass being created for other Yale buildings from 1919 through 1934. Despite Bonawit's enormous pro-ductivity at Yale and elsewhere, he remains a somewhat elusive figure in the history of

American stained glass and has never received due recognition.

Life

George Owen Bonawit was born February 28, 1891, in Brooklyn, New York, into an artistic family. His father, George Bonawitz, was an illustrator and designer with his own Manhattan studio. George Bonawitz was the fourth son of German immigrant parents who had settled in Brooklyn by at least 1854. Bonawitz married Margaret Mary Bowen, sister of Owen J. Bowen, a stained glass craftsman and partner of the well-known Otto Heinigke from 1890 through 1915. Both Young and Heinigke were leaders in the American stained glass movement who advocated the basic principles and methods of the Medieval stained glass craft as opposed to the opalescent Art Glass Movement lead by Tiffany and LaFarge. Both Heinigke & Bowen and Henry Wynd Young produced mosaic stained glass, largely for ecclesiastical settings.

George Owen Bonawit, known as G. Owen, became interested in stained glass through his father and his uncle, Owen Bowen, and spent much time in the workshop of Heinigke & Bowen. When Bonawit graduated from Pratt Institute in Brooklyn, he was proficient in the traditional method of fabricating stained glass. He was briefly associated with Henry Wynd Young in the firm of Young and Bonawit around 1914-1915 and carried out a large commission at this time. One of Bonawit's early mosaic stained glass windows of St. Louis of France was chosen by the Architectural League of New York to appear in their Annual Exhibition in 1917, a considerable honor in this field.

Bonawit also studied photography at the Modern School of Photography in New York City, and he served several months in the U.S. Army during World War I working with aerial photography.

By 1918, Bonawit had established his own firm, G. Owen Bonawit, Inc., in New York City. After offering a wide variety of interior decorative services, stained glass soon emerged as the primary focus for the firm. Although Bonawit would become a master of secular stained glass in the 1920s and 1930s, he often undertook ecclesiastical commissions. Proficient in both fields, he preferred the secular.

The Bonawit firm was highly successful by the late 1920s. G. Owen Bonawit married Janice Bowen, a distant relation on his mother's side, and they had two children. He and his family were able to move from Brooklyn to Ridgewood, New Jersey, in 1927, following his brother and parents who had moved there in 1920. James Gamble Rogers awarded Bonawit a large number of commissions for academic work, work that clearly demonstrated Bonawit's particular talent for producing glass decorations suitable to any setting, and Bonawit carried out many other commissions as well, many of them the result of competitive awards. His last great work following the Depression and World War II was the five large tower windows for the Church of the Ascension in New York City, a job that was a fitting and beautiful final statement.

Bonawit abruptly left New York City and the stained glass field in 1941 at the age of 50. Following a domestic upset and a divorce, Bonawit moved west and changed his focus to photography. He worked for Goodyear Aircraft of Arizona for several years and then entered government work as a scientific photographer covering the Southwest for the Interior Department's Bureau of Land Reclamation. He settled in Phoenix doing professional photography for the U.S. Government on the building of the Parker Dam. He next moved to White Sands, New Mexico, where he continued his photographic work at the White Sands Missile Range in the Technical Photographic Unit of the White Sands Integrated Range Mission. Upon his retirement in 1961, he returned to Phoenix and then to Miami, Florida. Bonawit died there in December of 1971 at the age of 80. He never returned to the stained glass field and made no attempt to maintain his ties with other stained glass craftsmen. When Bonawit closed his studio, he destroyed his records and sold whatever decorated glass remained. Although Bonawit was well respected as a stained glass artist, he was both shy and modest and not well known, even by his peers.

Early Churches

Early work was carried out by Bonawit with Henry Wynd Young in their firm of Young & Bonawit for the House of Hope Presbyterian

---

Upper left: Yale's largest decorated window by Bonawit faces High Street in the Branford Memorial Chapel. Made in the traditional Medieval style, it shows figures important in Man's intellectual development. **Upper right:** Branford College contains many Bonawit windows in its common rooms, including this astronomer, one of several Medieval figures done in the mosaic leaded style. **Lower left:** Yale's Saybrook College also contains Bonawit glass in its communal rooms, this one of a Medieval lady. The leaded decoration of the 18th Century lady (**lower right**) is typical of another Bonawit style.

Church in St. Paul, Minnesota. The beautiful, somewhat stylized figures in several windows installed there provided an excellent start for Bonawit's career. Another of Bonawit's early commissions was a large full-color stained glass window for the chancel in the Huguenot Memorial Church in Pelham, New York. Aspects of this window were to be repeated in the Harkness Tower at Yale a few years later. The composition, the unusually graceful style of the figures, and the border softened by the use of uneven or curved leading lines were characteristics that would be repeated in later work. Bonawit described this design as being in the "English fifteenth century style". Its sketch appeared in the catalog of a stained glass exhibit mounted by the Carnegie Institute in 1922.

Just over half of the 20 entries exhibited by Bonawit in the Carnegie show were of religious subjects, including several used in the Cleveland Cathedral and in St. Vincent de Ferrer's Church in New York City, and it was likely that most of Bonawit's early output was for ecclesiastical settings. However, the breadth of his entries, from early to late Gothic styles, French and English medallions, and the French grisaille glass of the 13th century, demonstrated the wide range of his expertise and his preference for medieval styles and subjects. All these styles were to be used in later commissions.

The Bonawit Firm

Bonawit established his firm of G. Owen Bonawit, Inc. by 1918. Located at various addresses in Manhattan, it was described by the terms "stained glass," "interior decorators," "leaded glass," and "glass stainers." Bonawit was the President, Manager, and Treasurer, and various relations served as other officers. In 1934, the firm had 15 employees, several of whom were designers and many of whom were Italian. Due to the "feast-or-famine" nature of this business, designers commonly moved from studio to studio, and it would be extremely difficult to identify the different hands in the output of any shop. Only two designers, Frederick Kurtz and the chief designer, Secord Charles Jaekle, have been identified as working largely for Bonawit. Kurtz also designed and painted most of the window decorations in Yale's Sterling Law Buildings for the Henderson

Brothers when Bonawit could not undertake the commission. Kurtz was involved in creating the windows under Otto Heinigke for the Cathedral of St. John the Divine in New York City.

Advertising in a few prestigious journals, the Bonawit firm became known by the leaded decorations used in these ads. These symbols included a hart pierced by an arrow, a galleon with banners flying, a mermaid in the Art Deco style, and a unicorn. Other publicity for Bonawit's work included captioned illustrations of his windows published in journals describing contemporary decorative trends.

Harkness House

Bonawit's first commission with the architect, James Gamble Rogers, which established the patron-architect-craftsman relationship so important for Yale later on, came in 1921 with the Harkness House window decorations in Manhattan. The house overlooked a narrow alley, and the two French doors on that side were filled with clouded glass covered with a patina wash obscuring the view. The Oriental-style designs showed birds, insects, and trees extending across the leaded panes. Fish decorated the bottom panels while birds flew across the upper part. Several small images, one of a spider and another of a Japanese sword guard, were to be repeated several years later in Yale's Sterling Library, as would the extension of designs over several panels and the use and placement of animal forms. These windows were an early example of Bonawit's creative style and flair for unusual but appropriate composition.

Yale's Harkness Memorial Quadrangle

James Gamble Rogers chose Bonawit to fabricate the window decorations for Yale's Harkness Memorial Quadrangle in 1921, a commission that established Bonawit's reputation for secular stained and leaded glass window decorations. Bonawit produced several types of glass decorations, exemplifying Rogers' belief that great variety of detail would provide both interest and an overall unity of feeling in the Gothic style used for these buildings. One window in every dormitory room had a painted quarry placed among the leaded panes, each vignette representing an aspect of college life at

These decorated windows in the original Edward Harkness House in New York City were crafted before 1922. The figures and format used here would be repeated in several other commissions by Bonawit, particularly the placement of birds at the top and of fish at the bottom of windows. Note the dangling spider on the right, a *trompe d'oeil* related to the 16th Century domestic glass of Europe.

Yale taken from old papers and scrapbooks. These scenes were refreshingly creative with touches of humor, similar in format to those used later in the Sterling Library. The Common Rooms contained more ambitious window decorations. Bonawit was proficient at decorative leadwork, and several doors in these rooms sported leaded galleons in their windows. Delicate lead figures of 18th century ladies and gentlemen served as focal points in one set of windows, with painted quarries scattered around them. Another room contained full-color mosaic leaded glass figures, including a stained glass painter, an attractive style not repeated by Bonawit elsewhere at Yale but that was to be used again with the same figures in a Michigan home (Alfred Wilson) in 1929.

The only large full-color mosaic stained glass window created by the Bonawit firm for Yale in the traditional ecclesiastical style was for the Memorial Room of the Harkness Tower. It was a tall four-light window comprised of eight life-size figures representing Euclid, Cicero, Herodotus, and others significant in the history of Man's intellectual development. The figures were in relaxed attitudes separated from each other by symbolic designs and medallions containing other figures; each light was edged by a colored glass border. The colors were bright and light rather than rich or deep and allowed the free entrance of natural light.

Cunard Building

Both the painted quarries and the mosaic figures used in Yale's Harkness Memorial Quadrangle were to be found in other early Bonawit work, notably the old Cunard Building windows in New York City. The six decorated windows which survive were installed in 1921 in two of the original Cunard Executive Offices. The leaded windows were profusely decorated with small painted subjects of aquatic life-forms, ships, and other sea-related scenes. A few larger colored mosaic figures of pirates stood out and were similar in technique to the mosaic figures in the Harkness Memorial Quadrangle. Another six full-color mosaic medallions depicted pirates against a background of William Morris-type foliage in bright colors. Three panes bear the name of the Bonawit firm, one of which is dated.

Private Work

The Bonawit firm provided stained glass decorations for many private residences during the 1920s, but most are difficult to locate or date exactly. Bonawit produced domestic glass and lead decorations for houses in Palm Beach; Detroit; Centenary, New York; Roslyn, Long Island; Ridgewood, New Jersey; and New York City as well as for many others not located. These windows were generally casement windows filled with diamond-shaped or rectangular leaded quarries. The small painted quarry was often the sole decoration. In other instances, mosaic figures and medallions, leaded figures, or large painted panels were installed.

Bonawit installed a whole series of painted medallions and leaded glass work in his own house in Ridgewood, New Jersey, after moving there in 1927. These images included at least 28 panels in four rooms, eight of Old King Cole and his entourage, galleons and hunters in lead, heraldic shields, birds, Dutch figures, and medieval rondels. They created a rich, lively decoration for the house that is very appealing.

Secular glass decorations for other public and private buildings were also crafted by the Bonawit firm during this period. Bonawit windows, now apparently lost, were located in an unidentified New York Club and in the now-demolished Park Lane Hotel. Designs for the latter were in the "Renaissance style of stained glass" with mosaic leaded figures placed across the top and a grapevine pattern extending over all the quarries in silver-gray tones. This style was directly related to examples of 15th and 16th century glass, especially grisaille work.

The move to decorate businesses, public buildings, schools, homes, and libraries with secular stained glass decorations was at its peak in the late 1920s and early 1930s. Several other American stained glass artists worked in this genre and general parallels with Bonawit's work can be drawn. While Bonawit was the master of the painted panel, most other artists used the mosaic leaded full-color technique. Henry Hunt, a Pittsburgh stained glass craftsman, produced work in the 1920s that was somewhat similar in draftsmanship and format. Wright Goodhue designed medallions in 1924 that were also comparable to work by Bonawit but that relied more on leading.

Upper left/right: The pirate, Long John Silver, his parrot and treasure chest are depicted in a window in the old Cunard Building in Manhattan, New York. **Lower left:** Nautical and marine images fill these Cunard windows including many ships such as this galleon. **Lower right:** The Cunard Steamship Line symbol graces one of the windows, Bonawit's 1921 signature is on others.

Charles J. Connick, a contemporary glass craftsman who was very popular for his ecclesiastical subjects, fabricated the secular window decorations for the Dining Hall at Kenyon College in Gambier, Ohio. A comparison of windows with similar themes by Connick and Bonawit showed the much greater liveliness and charm achieved by Bonawit. Although Bonawit was comfortable working with mosaic leaded glass for both secular and ecclesiastical subjects, Connick's windows demonstrated some of the disadvantages of the mosaic medallion as opposed to the painted panel for smaller subjects. The panel allowed the artist freedom in his painting and eliminated the leading of many small pieces of glass. It also avoided leading lines that could be awkward or too heavy for a small figure. Bonawit's use of the painted panel emphasized the pictorial qualities of these small decorations and lent a delicacy and richness to the images.

Bonawit produced ecclesiastical window designs throughout his stained glass career, but a telling comment appeared in the 1930 *Fortune* article that Bonawit "deals in modern manners and subjects and avoids church contracts as he would the deadly tarantula." This preference for secular subjects combined with a talent for matching the design and format of decorations to the style of the building made Bonawit particularly suited for carrying out the large commissions for academic institutions that came to him.

First Presbyterian Church

When a fire burned down the Chapel of the First Presbyterian Church of Wilmington, North Carolina, they brought in Bonawit to craft the new windows for the rebuilt chapel in 1928.

Grace Episcopal Church

Five stained glass windows in the Grace Episcopal Church in Colorado Springs, Colorado, were fabricated by the Bonawit firm and installed in 1930 and in 1939. The Church, built in 1925, was a fine example of the Gothic Revival, and the windows were significant examples of Bonawit's ecclesiastical stained glass. They included the great West Window and a series of four windows showing the life and teachings of Jesus. Other windows in the Church were designed by Henry Wynd Young,

Wilbur Burnham, and Clement Heaton.

Church of Bethesda-by-the-Sea

Bonawit installed windows in the Church of Bethesda-by-the-Sea in Palm Beach, Florida, some time between 1925 and 1933 when the building was completed. Built under the direction of Rector Russell, who had recently come from Washington's National Cathedral, this commission had strong ties with the search for the perfect windows for Washington Cathedral described later. Bonawit may have created the Bethesda-by-the-Sea windows after he traveled to Spain to view the Léon windows in 1933.

Yale's Sterling Memorial Library

At the request of Rogers, Bonawit fabricated the stained glass windows for the Sterling Memorial Library at Yale in 1930 and 1931. Bonawit would ultimately provide the window decorations for eight of the buildings at Yale, all designed by Rogers in the Gothic style. Bonawit rarely submitted bids for the work done at Yale; instead, he was invited by Rogers to present estimates. Bonawit was one of a select group of four artists who were assigned work in this way, the others being René Chambellan for the stone sculpture, Eugene Savage for the painting, and Samuel Yellin for the decorative ironwork. All other jobs required competitive bids from three or more companies with the lowest bidder awarded the contract. The architect's commitment to the best artists in each medium was illustrated by the competitive bids received for the decorative leaded glass in Davenport and Pierson colleges at Yale. Bonawit submitted a bid for these jobs, but his was the highest and more than four times higher than the winning bid. However, Bonawit's charges for the work he did carry out were consistently under the amount allowed for that item in the budget.

Bonawit produced painted panels for the second through the seventh floors of Yale's Sterling Memorial Library at $25 each. These medallions were delivered to the Henderson Brothers' New York City shop for insertion in the leaded windows before installation. The huge amount of decorated glass created by Bonawit for the ground and first mezzanine floors, however, was installed by the Bonawit firm and accounted for most of the cost to the

University. Yale paid Bonawit a total of $255,389 for all the Library's "Special Glass" while the Henderson Brothers received $28,532 for the "Typical Glass."

At this same time in 1930/31, Yale's Sterling Law School buildings, also designed by Rogers, were under construction. Rogers felt that Bonawit was too busy with the Library windows to handle the glass decorations for the Law School buildings and so recommended that a local New Haven firm (for the typical glass) and the Henderson Brothers be awarded the job. Many of the glass decorations varied in technique and style from Bonawit's work, but a large number of designs were indistinguishable. These included the series of 32 "Vanity Fair judges" in the main stairwell and the many playing card figures. One of Bonawit's main designers, Frederick Kurtz, also worked for the Henderson Brothers during this period, which explained the similarity in style and the overall continuity between the buildings.

Yale's Hall of Graduate Studies

Bonawit carried out the last of his large Yale commissions for the Hall of Graduate Studies, designed by Rogers and opened in 1932. The artist again used the painted panel and the mosaic heraldic shields as well as a few leaded clear glass outline designs in medallions that complemented the nearby painted panels. Bonawit created 50 panels, mostly of classical subjects, for the Dining Hall, while the Lounge was decorated with 77 painted glass medallions representing various disciplines in the curriculum of the Graduate School. The Lounge windows were less restrained in stylistic treatment than were those in the Sterling Library. Bonawit was evidently given a free hand to create imaginative designs in broad subject areas. Many images represented natural forms that become patterns, and several showed a bold creative energy appropriate to the natural sciences. Humorous and even macabre touches were seen here, and one design exceeded the bounds of the panel. A few images were painted in the Art Deco style, and several repeated early printing subjects and the Jost Amman occupations that also appeared in the Library. Heraldic shields, figures in lead, and painted panels bordered by pot-metal colored glass were to be found in the

Hall of Graduate Studies windows, although none of the smaller painted quarries were used.

Northwestern University's Deering Library

Secular window decorations for the Charles Deering Library at Northwestern University outside Chicago were crafted by Bonawit in 1932. Another Gothic building designed by Rogers, the Deering Library was decorated with 70 painted panels illustrating broad fields of learning with an emphasis on American history. The subjects were designed primarily by Bonawit who did considerable research for each design. Bonawit's notes, deposited in the Library Archives at Northwestern, revealed his knowledge of a wide range of topics and his close attention to detail. The format of these decorations was similar to that used in Yale's Sterling Library, although mosaic medallions appeared more often at Northwestern.

Girard College Chapel

Also in 1932, the Bonawit firm produced the windows for the Chapel of Girard College, a Philadelphia boys school. The Girard commission required a competitive entry, and four stained glass artists were invited to enter: Bonawit, Nicola D'Ascenzo, Henry Lee Willet, and Oliver Smith, Otto Heinigke's partner after the death of Owen J. Bowen. The building was in the Greek Revival architectural style with 30 octagonal window openings in each of the 26 windows. Bonawit designed a simple Greek motif in amber glass covered with gold for the decoration, and this was deemed best suited to the setting. The College officials grudgingly awarded the contract to an out-of-town firm because Bonawit's windows "were so conspicuously desirable". Even the architects expressed their admiration for "the masterful way in which he [Bonawit] has fulfilled his task."

Duke University Chapel

Bonawit carried out a large commission for Duke University in 1931-33 as the sole fabricator of stained glass for the Duke University Chapel. The Chapel's 73 mosaic window designs were interpretations of Biblical stories in the Medieval manner. Over 800 figures were represented in the windows, 301 of them larger-than-life size. The Noah window is signed by Bonawit. The

Over Left: This oddly interesting image of a skeleton and a giant spider represents one of the scientific disciplines taught in Yale's Graduate School; it appears in the Lounge of the Hall of Graduate Studies.
Over Right: Bonawit's tendency towards Art Deco so apparent in the Sterling Memorial Library (in particular over the entrance door and in the Newspaper Reading Room) can be seen in this image from the corridor outside the Lounge in Yale's Hall of Graduate Studies.

smaller Memorial Chapel windows contained complicated patterns in white grisaille glass, and the number of pieces used in these windows was "probably over a million". The Chapel's architecture was English Gothic, but the windows were based on the medieval French style of the 12th and 13th centuries. The Duke windows firmly established Bonawit's reputation in the ecclesiastical stained glass field. This competitive contract was reportedly for $100,000, a considerable sum at the height of the Depression.

Yale Residential Colleges

Rogers again chose Bonawit as the window artist for many of the residential colleges at Yale during the early 1930s. The Bonawit firm provided all the "special leaded glass work" which included a few painted panels for Berkeley College, built in 1934. Special leading and other ornamental glass by Bonawit were installed in Trumbull College in 1932/33, when the Henderson Brothers again did the "typical glass" work. Bonawit undertook the "special glass and glazing" for Jonathan Edwards College in 1932, and when the Harkness Memorial Quadrangle was renovated in 1932/33 and divided into Branford and Saybrook colleges, the Bonawit firm carried out the "special glazing" required to maintain the decorative continuity within the original buildings.

Also built in 1932, Calhoun College was one of the buildings at Yale designed by Rogers but that did not have window decorations by Bonawit. At Calhoun, the stained glass was fabricated by Nicola D'Ascenzo, a craftsman popular for his religious glass who had produced the mosaic stained glass windows for Dwight Hall when it was renovated in 1932. D'Ascenzo followed Bonawit's format with the 70 painted panels for the college dining hall, library, and Commons Room with subjects appropriate to the college. However, his painting is less finely detailed than that of Bonawit's as he did not use the stick-work technique, and he employed more colored paints, making some of the panels look garish.

Foreign Work

Although few details are known, Bonawit carried out commissions for window decorations in the Palace of the King of Siam in Bangkok, and for the decorative leaded windows in the Ambassador's residence at the U.S. Embassy in Tokyo, Japan. Windows for the latter contract, probably fabricated in 1930/31 but now lost, were evidently made to resemble a Japanese screen with milky translucent glass, gold covered bars, and golden chrysanthemums at the intersections.

European Trip

In 1933, Bonawit was sent to see the windows of Léon Cathedral in Spain as one of the eight "glass painters" asked to analyze and report on the glass by the Fine Arts Committee of Washington's National Cathedral. The Committee was searching for the perfect style of stained glass windows to install in the National Cathedral. Léon was thought to have the "most beautiful" and "lightest full colored windows" of any European cathedral. Léon and Washington were situated at the same latitude and, therefore, experienced approximately the same light intensity. This was Bonawit's first trip to Europe, and he was clearly impressed by the Léon windows, the trip leading him to modify his style of stained glass fabrication in later religious settings.

Ecclesiastical Work

Bonawit turned in earnest to the fabrication of ecclesiastical stained glass in the early to mid-1930s and produced many windows beyond the Duke commission. His larger mosaic windows of religious subjects were colorful and competitive with the work of his peers, although his secular creations were more inventive and lively. The exception may be Bonawit's final magnificent work for New York City's Church of the Ascension.

This change of focus from the secular to the ecclesiastical glass field came as the result of many factors. There was a decline in the demand for domestic window decorations in the 1930s since the new architectural styles bore no relation to the Gothic, and the functional tended to push out the decorative. Also, the severe economic conditions of the Depression, particularly after 1933, forced a cutback in all residential and commercial decorations, and many stained glass craftsmen were forced out of business.

Bonawit produced many ecclesiastical

Upper: Northwestern University's Gothic Charles Deering Library contains the McCormick-Deering harvester in a window. **Lower left:** Black Hawk from Northwestern's Deering Library. **Lower right:** Funded by the Harkness family, the non-denominational Chapel on the Connecticut College campus in New London is decorated throughout with Bonawit windows. Note his name and date at lower left.

Ma'Katawimesheka'Ka.

B.OWEN
DESIGNER   BONAWI
          MAKE
19 NEW   YORK 30

works during the Depression, several far from New York City. A New England example of Bonawit's religious work termed "excellent" by a peer is in the old Trinity Church in Concord, Massachusetts. Bonawit windows were also installed in Christ Church, Cranbrook, Michigan, and Bonawit carried out a second commission for the great west window for Grace Episcopal Church in Colorado Springs in 1939. Back in New York City, he fabricated several large windows for Temple Emanu-El on Fifth Avenue.

The start of World War II marked the demise of the secular glass business and it severely limited the production of any glass for religious settings. By 1940, many of the glassmen who had survived the Depression went out of business when the War effort restricted materials and drafted glass workers.

Church of the Ascension
One of Bonawit's last commissions was the stained glass for the large tower windows in the Church of the Ascension on Fifth Avenue at 10th Street, called one of the greatest commissions in stained glass of New York City. A friend of Rector Donald Aldrich, Bonawit had already designed and installed four small mosaic windows in the All Soul's Chapel in 1938/39. Other windows in the church contained stained glass in the opalescent style made popular by John LaFarge and D. Maitland Armstrong. In contrast, Bonawit filled the five large tower windows with richly colored mosaic glass in the Medieval style. Refreshing and highly successful, these windows illustrated Biblical stories with 123 scenes, each identified by the Bible reference. The format suggested the Medieval windows of Chartres Cathedral, though the exact scheme was not copied. However, this commission was related in style to the work done for Duke University in the early 1930s. Rich in deep blues, bright reds, and golden yellows with purple and green accents, the figures were drawn in the Medieval style with strong-lined features, wide-open eyes, and Gothic draperies. Each window was signed by "G. Owen Bonawit, Designer and Maker, 1941." The fact that Bonawit signed his own name and that he alone installed the windows indicated that he was working alone by this time.

Summary
Bonawit and his firm produced stained glass for both secular and ecclesiastical installations that was outstanding for its variety, beauty, quality, and style in the American stained glass movement of the 1920s and 1930s. His versatility was demonstrated not only through the wide variety of decorative forms of his glass but in his creative interpretation of designs that captured an energy and liveliness unusual in the field. Bonawit's personal artistic style was often "modern" with an Art Deco flavor, showing the influence of popular trends in other artistic media through stylized decorative figures and patterns. However, he welcomed all styles of stained glass from all periods, and his interpretation of the Medieval was superb.

The majority of Bonawit's work was designed to fit a specific setting and was crafted in an appropriate style. At the same time, Cubism, the Bauhaus, and other abstract styles were influencing secular stained glass elsewhere, but the Gothic revival in the United States, especially for academic institutions, provided the perfect environment in which an artist such as Bonawit could excel.

Trained in traditional Medieval methods and styles, Bonawit chose to concentrate on the domestic glass field, so popular during the 1920s and early 1930s. It is probable that the Bonawit firm was one of the largest producers of secular stained glass decorations during this time in the United States, and Bonawit had considerable influence on the popularity of this form through architects such as James Gamble Rogers and the many universities built in the Gothic style. Bonawit was a master of secular glass, and, though he has received little subsequent notice, he was recognized by his contemporaries as one of the finest craftsmen of his time. His work stands as a brilliant testimony to that talent.

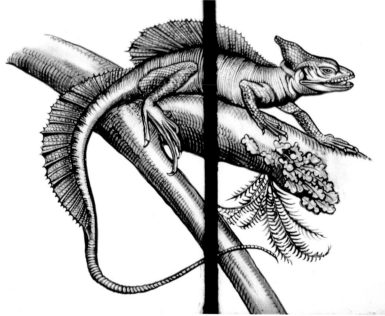

Upper left/right: The Church of the Ascension in New York City boasts five beautiful tower windows by Bonawit done in the Medieval style of Chartres Cathedral. Dating from 1940 and 1941, the 123 scenes from the Bible are marked with the reference. Note Bonawit's name and date in the top images.
Lower left/right: The lizard shown at upper right and at bottom left was one of many animals used repeatedly by Bonawit. At lower right is the same lizard from Room 335 in Yale's Sterling Library.

LOCATIONS OF BONAWIT WINDOWS

All known locations of Bonawit glass are listed along with the name of the building or owner at the time of installation, the location, the type of window or decorations, the date installed when known, and the reference identifying each location (see the list following for the references).

Berkeley College, New Haven, Connecticut, see **Yale University**.

Bethesda-by-the-Sea, Palm Beach, Florida, see **Church of Bethesda-by-the-Sea**.

1. <u>Mr. Edward **Bok**</u>, Lake Wales, Florida. Painted windows with aquatic subjects, installed before 1931. (Ref.: *Fortune*, v. 2:6, Dec. 1930, p. 80.)

2. <u>Mr. G. Owen **Bonawit**</u>, 333 West End Avenue, Ridgewood, New Jersey. Decorated windows through-out artist's home, a total of at least 28 windows in 4 rooms: 4 images of decorative leading only, 4 of leaded mosaic heraldic shields, and 19 painted panels, many of which relate to work done elsewhere (Bonawit lived here from at least 1933 to 1941). (Ref.: Peggy Bonawit Labash correspondence.)

Bowling Green Branch, U.S. Post Office, New York City, New York, see **Cunard Building**.

Branford College, New Haven, Connecticut, see **Yale University**.

Branford Memorial Chapel, New Haven, Connecticut, see **Yale University**.

Charles Deering Library, Evanston, Illinois, see **Northwestern University**.

3. **Christ Church**, Cranbrook, Michigan. Aisle window of unknown date; architect was Bertram Grosvenor Goodhue Associates. (Ref.: Connick, *Adventures in Light and Color*, p. 371.)

4. **Church of Bethesda-by-the-Sea**, Palm Beach, Florida. Three signed Bonawit windows installed between 1927 and 1933. (Ref.: Church personnel; Dorothy Bonawit Nagel correspondence.)

5. **Church of St. Vincent de Ferrer**, 66th and Lexington, New York City. Windows designed for the St. Joseph's Chapel in 1922 or earlier. Architect was Bertram Grosvenor Goodhue (one of Goodhue's "finest Gothic facades"). (Ref.: Carnegie Institute, *Stained Glass Exhibition*, 1922, p. 5.)

6. **Church of the Ascension**, Fifth Avenue and West Tenth Street, New York City. Two 1' x 3' windows installed in All Soul's Chapel in 1938, two more in 1939, all on the life of Christ. Five large tower win-dows were installed at the eastern end of the sanctuary depicting 123 scenes from the Bible from the Story of the Creation to that of Judas Maccabeus, each identified with chapter and verse. One window was fabricated in 1940-1941, the rest in 1941, and all were installed by Bonawit in 1941. Done in a mosaic pot-metal style with Medieval inspiration. Architect was Richard Upjohn, renovated by McKim, Mead and White. (Ref.: visit; Church secretary; Willet interview; Henderson correspondence.)

7. **Cleveland Cathedral**, Cleveland, Ohio. Bonawit's windows in the east chancel and sanctuary were designed before 1922. (Ref.: Carnegie Institute, *Stained Glass Exhibition*, 1922, p. 5.)

Commonwealth Fund, New York City, New York, see **Harkness House**.

8. **Connecticut College, Harkness Chapel** (Interdenominational), New London, Connecticut. Sixteen large windows (two are semi-circles) of Biblical subjects installed 1939 with several hundred painted

quarries, includes 14 mosaic leaded scenes, and 2 mosaic leaded rose windows; architect was James Gamble Rogers. Rogers "secured some extra panes for the stained glass windows of Harkness Chapel" that were sent to President Blunt June 19, 1942, and stored in the Business Manager's office for safe-keeping until needed for replacement. (Ref.: visit; dedication program and descriptive flyer, clipping in Connecticut College files; Connecticut College Librarian Brian Rogers.)

9. **Cranbrook Museum**, Cranbrook, Michigan. Panel of "Christopher Columbus" of unknown date. (Ref.: Connick, *Adventures in Light and Color*, p. 371.)

10. **Cunard Building**, Executive Offices (originally included Saloon Passengers' Lounge), 25 Broadway, New York City (now Bowling Green Branch, U.S. Post Office and private offices). Six windows in two rooms (at present) of sea scenes, pirates, ships, and fish. Installed in 1921; architect was Benjamin Wistar Morris. (Ref.: visit; *House Beautiful*, v. 52, Sept. 1922, pp. 214-215, 249.)

Deering Library, Evanston, Illinois, see **Northwestern University**.

11. Mrs. Horace **Dodge**, Detroit, Michigan. Painted and leaded casement windows. Installed before 1928. (Ref.: *Arts and Decoration*, v. 28:4, Feb. 1928, p. 74.)

12. **Duke University Chapel** and **Memorial Chapel**, Durham, North Carolina. All 72 large windows in the main Chapel are by Bonawit and represent Biblical scenes; his windows in the Memorial Chapel are done in the grisaille style; there are decorative lead and gold symbols for the doors. Installed in 1932, architect was Horace Trumbauer. (Ref.: Blackburn, *Architecture of Duke University*; Connick, *Adventures in Light and Color*, p.367; Duke Archives correspondence.)

13. Country house in **Essex Fells**, New Jersey. Unidentified location. Wrought lead door, installed before 1931. (Ref.: *Arts and Decoration*, v. 35, no. 3, July 1931, p. 53.)

14. **First National Bank and Trust Company Building**, Hamilton, Ohio. Lead and glass over entrance. Childs & Smith were the architects. The Lindon Company hired Bonawit. (Ref.: *Architecture*, v.65:1, Jan. 1932, p.16 and Feb. 1931.)

15. **First Presbyterian Church**, 125 S. 3rd St., Wilmington, North Carolina. The Chapel windows, probably installed in 1928. (Ref.: Church personnel, Leslie N. Boney, Jr., architect, correspondence; Dreck Wilson correspondence; *Let There be Light*. - Wilmington, NC, First Presbyterian Church, 1990).

16. **Girard College Chapel**, Philadelphia, Pennsylvania. Twenty-six ocyagonal window designs employing gold leaf on amber glass. Installed in 1932. (Ref.: Raymond I. Haskell, "On Visiting the Girard College Chapel"; College correspondence.)

17. **Grace Episcopal Church,** Colorado Springs, Colorado. Aisle windows installed 1930-1938, great west window installed 1939; later windows by Bonawit, earlier ones by Young and Bonawit. Architects were Frohman, Robb and Little. (Ref.: Church leaflet; Dorothy Bonawit Nagel correspondence; Connick, *Adventures in Light and Color*, p. 375.)

Hall of Graduate Studies, New Haven, Connecticut, see **Yale University**.

18. **Hampton Shops**, Living-Hall, Hampton Building, 18 E. 50th Street, New York City. Tentative identification. Painted medallions in at least two leaded windows showing same images used elsewhere by Bonawit. (Ref.: *Arts & Decoration*, v. 28:3, ad.)

19. **Hardware Mutual Insurance Building**, Stevens Point, Wisconsin. Leaded glass panels in Board of Directors Room and private offices. Architects were Childs & Smith; Bonawit hired by the Lindon Company. (Ref.: *Architecture*, Oct. 1922 and Jan. 1932, p. 16.)

Harkness Chapel, New London, Connecticut, see **Connecticut College**.

20. **Mr. and Mrs. Edward S. Harkness House** (built in 1906-08, now The Commonwealth Fund), One East 75th Street, New York City. Two windows of painted scenes with Oriental influence, installed before 1922. (Ref.: visit; *House Beautiful*, v. 52, Sept. 1922, pp. 214-215, 249.)

Harkness Memorial Quadrangle, New Haven, Connecticut, see **Yale University**.

21. **Mr. Gordon P. Henderson**, Towaco, New Jersey. Had a "few painted and fired ship panels from Leo Popper & Sons". The remaining glass in Bonawit's Studio went to Popper in 1941 and then to Alliance Art Glass. (Ref.: Edwin Popper correspondense; Gordon Henderson correspondence; Bruegger at Alliance Art Glass.)

22. **House of Hope Presbyterian Church**, St. Paul, Minnesota. The Apocalypse Window, the Mary and Martha Window, and the Ministry of Healing Window were all done by Young and Bonawit, installed in 1914-1915. Architect was Ralph Adam Cram. (Ref.: visit; Dorothy Bonawit Nagel correspondence; Church booklet.)

23. **Huguenot Memorial Church**, Pelham, New York. Described as "English 15th Century," Bonawit's chancel windows were probably installed around 1919-20. (Ref.: Architectural League of New York, *Annual Exhibition*, 1920; Carnegie Institute, *Stained Glass Exhibition*, 1922, p. 5.)

24. **Independence Hall**, Philadelphia, Pennsylvania. At least one panel - in honor of and showing a portrait of Wendell L. Willkie. (Ref.: photocopy in the Hornung Eagle Collection in Slides & Prints, Yale University; Peggy Bonawit Labash correspondence; newspaper clipping.)

Jonathan Edwards College, New Haven, Connecticut, see **Yale University**.

25. **Mr. Sam Katz**, Centenary, New York. Leaded figure in the bar; installed before 1931. (Ref.: *Fortune*, v. 2:6, Dec. 1930, p. 78.)

26. **King of Siam Palace**, Bangkok, Thailand. Unknown style, unknown date. (Ref.: Dorothy Bonawit Nagel correspondence; newspaper clipping.)

27. **Mr. Charles Thompson Matthews**, (224 West 149th Street?), New York City. Painted panels, installed before 1928 at least in the Breakfast Room. (Ref.: *Arts and Decoration*, v. 28:4, Feb. 1928, p. 74.)

Meadow Brook Hall, Rochester, Michigan, see **Wilson**.

Memorial Chapel, Duke University, Durham, North Carolina, see **Duke University**.

Michigan State University, see **Wilson**.

28. A **New York City Club**, unidentified. Leaded and painted window in the dining room in the manner of English stained glass (includes 9 large leaded medallions). (Ref.: *Arts and Decoration*, v. 35:4, Aug. 1931, p. 55.)

Upper left: G. Owen Bonawit as an art student at Pratt Institute of Art in New York, between 1910 and 1918. **Upper right:** Bonawit, probably in the early 1930s, at his father's in the Catskills. **Lower left:** Bonawit at about 43 (in 1934). **Lower right:** A picture of Bonawit taken in 1961 when he was 70 years old. (All four pictures courtesy of Peggy Bonawit Labash, his daughter.)

29. **New York World's Fair**, 1939-40. Unidentified work. Probably in Temple of Religion? Possibly subsequently owned by Rubey Brookshire of Colorado Springs, CO. (Ref.: NYPL Art and Architecture Reference Division files.)

30. **Northern States Life Insurance Building**, Hammond, Indiana. Painted panels and ornamental leaded doors installed before 1928. Childs & Smith were the architects. (Ref.: Stained Glass Association of America, *Bulletin*, v. 23:7, Aug. 1928, pp. 9-10; *Architecture*, v. 65:1, Jan. 1932, p. 17.)

31. **Northwestern University, Charles Deering Library**, including Music Library, Transportation Library, Liberal Arts Reserve Room, Evanston, Illinois. Painted and mosaic panels of American History and other subjects, 70 in all, fabricated and installed in 1932. James Gamble Rogers was the architect. (Ref.: visit; "Old West in Stained Glass," Minneapolis Art Institute, *Bulletin*; file in Northwestern Library Archives.)

32. **Old Trinity Church**, Concord, Massachusetts. Chancel and side chancel windows, one representing St. Cecelia. Unknown date but probably 1921. (Ref.: Skinner, Orin E., "Stained Glass Tours - New England," in Stained Glass Association of America, *Bulletin*, vol. 61:4, 1966/67, p.37.)

33. **Park Lane Hotel** (36 Central Park South, New York City, demolished in the late 1950's). Windows, both leaded panels and painted/stained designs, at least in apartment of Fullerton Weaver, installed before 1931. (Ref.: *Arts & Decoration*, vol. 35:4, Aug. 1931, p. 55.)

34. Residence in **Roslyn**, Long Island, New York. Unidentified location. Decorative leading, installed before 1928. (Ref.: *Arts and Decoration*, v. 28:6, April 1928, pp. 73, 112.)

35. **St. Bartholomew's Church**, Park Avenue, New York City. Window designed in 1922 or earlier. Architect was Bertram Grosvenor Goodhue. (Ref.: Carnegie Inst., *Stained Glass Exhibition*, 1922, p. 5.)

St. Vincent de Ferrer Church, New York City, New York, see **Church of St. Vincent de Ferrer**.

Saybrook College, New Haven, Connecticut, see **Yale University**.

36. Mr. Charles M. **Schwab**, New York City. Painted medallions in leaded and painted casements, installed before 1928. (Ref.: *Arts and Decoration*, v. 28:4, Feb. 1928, p. 74.)

37. Mr. Dudley S. **Sieler**, 15 E. 80th St., New York City. Tentative identification. Hart pierced through the throat with an arrow and other small painted decorations in leaded casement windows in living room. (Unattributed in Architectural League of New York, *Annual Exhibition*, 1922, p. 25.)

Sterling Memorial Library, New Haven, Connecticut, see **Yale University**.

38. **Swedish American Line, S.S. Gripsholm and S.S. Stockholm**, passenger liners. Bonawit glass probably in sky-light domes of dining rooms. (Ref.: Peggy Bonawit Labash correspondence.)

39. **Taft School**, Watertown, Connecticut. Many panels (32) and leaded and painted quarries in the Old Library and other rooms in Taft Hall showing early printers' and printmakers' marks, school insignias, and other education-related subjects. James Gamble Rogers was the architect. (Ref.: visit; no printed reference but preponderance of evidence from similar style and subjects.)

40. **Temple Emanu-El**, 521 Fifth Avenue, New York City. Window installed around 1929. (Ref.: visit; Dorothy Bonawit Nagel correspondence; Connick, *Adventures in Light and Color*, p. 357.)

Trumbull College, New Haven, Connecticut, see **Yale University**.

41. <u>**U.S. Embassy, Ambassador's Residence**</u>, Tokyo, Japan. Decorative leaded windows, silhouette work in lead on glass. Completed in 1931, the windows are no longer extant. Architect was H. Van Buren Magonigle. (Ref.: Dorothy Bonawit Nagel correspondence; *Architecture*, v. 65:1, Jan. 1932, p.16; Peggy Bonawit Labash correspondence.)

    U.S. Post Office, Bowling Green Branch, New York City, New York, see **Cunard Building**.

    University Chapel, Duke University, Durham, North Carolina, see **Duke University**.

42. <u>Ms. R. G. **Walker**</u>, Wilsonville, Oregon. Ten stained and painted medallions in the collection of the author, from Alliance Art Glass, New York City, purchased in 1979 and 1998.

43. <u>**West Side Presbyterian Church**</u>, 6 South Monroe Street, Ridgewood, New Jersey. Stained glass made for the church probably while Bonawit resided in Ridgewood in the 1920s and 1930s. (Ref.: Peggy Bonawit Labash; Ridgewood newspaper clipping from 1940; Lincoln Stulik correspondence.)

44. <u>Mr. and Mrs. Alfred G. **Wilson**</u>, Meadow Brook Hall, Rochester, Michigan (now belongs to Michigan State University), completed in 1929 based on 16th and 17th century English manor house style. At least 7 full-color pot metal leaded windows in rectangular panels depicting medieval occupations, including a stained glass painter, in the library. Designed by the Tiffany Studios, made by the G. Owen Bonawit Studio. Building designed by William E. Kapp of the Detroit firm of Smith, Hinchman and Grylls. (Ref.: Michigan Stained Glass Census, window for March 1999.)

45. <u>**Yale University, Branford College**</u>, 74 High Street, New Haven, Connecticut. Decorative painted quarries in every student room, 9 mosaic leaded figures and 9 painted quarries in the two Common Rooms, all installed in 1933, and one large four-light leaded mosaic window (largest Bonawit window on campus) in the Memorial Room of the Harkness Tower. Architect was James Gamble Rogers. (Ref.: visit; Yale records.)

46. <u>**Yale University, Berkeley College**</u>, 205 Elm Street, New Haven, Connecticut. Decorative leading and about 5 painted panels, installed in 1934. Architect was James Gamble Rogers. (Ref.: Visit; Yale records.)

47. <u>**Yale University, Hall of Graduate Studies**</u>, 320 York Street, New Haven, Connecticut. Painted panels, mosaic panels, leaded figures - at least 258 decorative windows installed in 1931-32. Architect was James Gamble Rogers. (Ref.: visit; Yale records; articles, etc.)

48. <u>**Yale University, Harkness Memorial Quadrangle**</u>, New Haven, Connecticut. Built in 1921/22 and designed by James Gamble Rogers, the Quadrangle was divided into the Branford and Saybrook residential Colleges in 1932/33. The Harkness Memorial Tower containing a large Bonawit window became associated with Branford College. (Ref.: visit; Yale records, etc.)

49. <u>**Yale University, Jonathan Edwards College**</u>, 68 High Street, New Haven, Connecticut. Six painted quarries relating to Jonathan Edwards along with decorative leading in the Curtiss Library. Installed in 1932. Architect was James Gamble Rogers. (Ref.: visit; Yale records.)

50. <u>**Yale University, Saybrook College**</u>, 242 Elm Street, New Haven, Connecticut. Decorative painted quarries in every student room, the Master's House, and the Hall. Twenty mosaic stained and decorative leaded panels and 6 painted quarries in two common rooms. Installed 1933; architect was

James Gamble Rogers. (Ref.: visit; Yale records.)

51. **Yale University, Sterling Memorial Library**, 120 High Street, New Haven, Connecticut. Quarry paintings, painted panels, mosaic shields, painted cabinet doors, leadwork decorations, lead-covered brass figures (679 panels, 160 leaded shields, 38 free-form paintings, 2,424 painted quarries). Installed 1930-31. Architects were James Gamble Rogers and Bertram Grosvenor Goodhue. There may be a panel in the Ashmun Street Physical Plant Office taken from a Yale building. (Ref.: visit; *Yale University Library Gazette*, April 1931; Yale records; articles, etc.)

52. **Yale University, Trumbull College**, 241 Elm Street, New Haven, Connecticut. Decorative glass and glazing, installed 1932-33. Architect was James Gamble Rogers. (Ref.: visit; Yale invoice, etc.)

(Possible location: <u>Hoboken Train Station</u>, Hoboken, New Jersey. Stained glass windows, discovered during renovation of the old station in 1999 when painted-over windows were uncovered. Attributed to Tiffany in the Press but Bonawit possibly involved. Undated. Ref.: Peggy Bonawit Labash.)

SELECTED BIBLIOGRAPHY

Almy, Ruth. "A Stained Glass Tour of Colorado. Part II. Outside Denver." In Stained Glass Association of America. *Bulletin*, Autumn 1971, pp. 13-19.

Architectural League of New York. *Annual Exhibition*. 1917, 1920-1931, 1933, 1938.

Blackburn, William. *The Architecture of Duke University*. Durham: Duke University Press, 1937.

Bonawit, G. Owen. "A Short Essay on Stained Glass." In The Woman's Club of Ridgewood N.J. *Bulletin*, vol. 8:3, Dec. 1935.

Bonawit, G. Owen. "St. Louis, King of France. Designed and Executed by G. Owen Bonawit, N.Y." In Architectural League of New York. *Annual Exhibition*, 1917, p. 48.

Bonawit, Oby J. *Book of Bonawitz and Bonewitz*. Revised. Miami, Florida, April, 1968.

Brooklyn City and Business Directory. Brooklyn: Lain & Co., 1870/71-1897/98.

Burnham, Wilbur Herbert. "Editorial Notes." In Stained Glass Association of America. *Bulletin*, vol. 37:2, Spring 1942, pp. 1-3.

Carnegie Institute. Fine Arts Department. *Stained Glass Exhibition*. Nov. 13 - Dec. 16, 1922. Pittsburgh, 1922.

Connick, Charles J. *Adventures in Light and Color*. Forward by Charles D. Maginnis. New York: Random House, 1937.

Connick, Charles J. "Modern Glass - A Review." In *International Studio*, vol. 80:329, Oct. 1924, pp. 40-53.

Day, Lewis F. *Stained Glass*. London: Chapman & Hall, 1903.

Day, Lewis F. *Windows. A Book about Stained and Painted Glass*. 3rd ed., rev. and enlarged. London: B. T. Batsford, 1909.

"Decoration of the Sterling Memorial Library." In *Yale University Library Gazette*, vol. 5:4, April 1931, pp. 81-123.

Directory of Directors in the City of New York. New York, 1919/20-1941.

Finch, Arthur. "Stained Glass for Home Decoration." In *House Beautiful*, vol. 54, Nov. 1923, pp. 478-79, 524, 526.

French, Robert Dudley, comp. *The Memorial Quadrangle. A Book about Yale*. New Haven: Yale University Press, 1930.

Goodyear, William H. "The Memorial Quadrangle and the Harkness Memorial Tower at Yale." In *American Architect*, vol. 120:2379, Oct. 26, 1921, pp. 299-314.

Haas, Arline de. "Notable Workers in Stained Glass Who Have Contributed to Art in America." In Stained Glass Association of America. *Bulletin*, vol. 18:11, Dec. 1924, p. 10.

Hale, William Harlan. "Art vs. Yale University." In *The Harkness Hoot*, vol. 1:2, Nov. 15, 1930, pp. 17-32.

Heaton, Clement. "The Art of Stained and Painted Glass." In *American Architect*, vol. 101:1881, Jan. 10, 1912, pp. 13-19, and following issues.

Heaton, Maurice. "Progressive Steps in the Making of Stained Glass Windows." In *American Architect*, vol. 135:2561, Jan. 20, 1929, pp. 97-103.

Heinigke, Otto. "Architectural Sympathy in Leaded Glass." In Stained Glass Association of America. *Bulletin*, vol. 32:1, Spring-Summer 1937, pp. 5-14.

Herrick, Cheesman A. "Girard College Chapel. " Address given by Herrick, May 19, 1940.

Holden, Reuben A. *Yale: A Pictorial History*. New Haven: Yale University Press, 1967.

Hunt, Henry. "Medallion in Nursery Window by Mr. Henry Hunt." In Stained Glass Association of America. *Bulletin*, vol. 24:8, Aug. 1929, pp. 6-7.

Karnaghan, Anne Webb. "Three Workers in Stained Glass." In *Magazine of Art*, vol. XIX, no. 11, Nov. 1928, pp. 588-596.

Keogh, Andrew. "Notes by the Librarian Based on an Address on Alumni Day 1928." In *Yale University Library Gazette*, vol. 3:1, July 1929, pp. 27-34.

McCloy, Helen. "A Lost Art Re-Born." In *Parnassus*, vol. 7:3, March 1935, pp. 4-6.

"Made by one of our Eastern Members." In Stained Glass Association of America. *Bulletin*, vol. 15:7, Aug. 1921, pp. 4-5.

Martin, Mary. "Stained, Leaded and Painted Glass." In *Arts & Decoration*, vol. 28:6, April 1928, pp. 73, 112.

"Modern Stained Glass." In *Fortune*, vol. 2:6, Dec. 1930, pp. 74-83.

New York Times; vol. 31:2, Sept. 6, 1951, and vol. 23:2, April 24, 1953. Obituaries (Henry and David J. Bonawit).

"Old West in Stained Glass." Minneapolis Institute of Arts. *Bulletin*, vol. 22:2, Jan. 14, 1933, pp. 10-11.

"Painted and Leaded Windows in New Designs." In *Arts & Decoration*, vol. 35:4, Aug. 1931, p. 55.

Residential Colleges at Yale University. 3rd ed. Edited by Richard C. Carroll. New Haven: Office of the Secretary, Yale University, 1977, p. 22.

Rogers, James Gamble. "The Sterling Memorial Library." In *Yale University Library Gazette*, vol. 3:1, July 1928.

Rogers, James Gamble. "Scrapbook containing postcards collected and used as sources for inspiration for designs for Yale buildings." Yale Art Library.

Rogers, James Gamble III. "James Gamble Rogers - Yale Architect." New Haven, April 30, 1968, typescript.

Sheldon, James. *Stained Glass*. Reprinted from the Summer Edition of *Religion in Life*, 1938, pp. 416-426.

Sheldon, James, comp. *Stained Glass at Washington Cathedral*. Washington: For the Fine Arts Committee as a Fact-finding Commission, 1927-1936.

Sheldon, James. "Two Schools of Stained Glass." In *The Cathedral Age*, vol. 14:1, Spring 1939, pp. 21-24.

Skinner, Orin E. "Stained Glass Dinner Meeting in New York." In Stained Glass Association of America. *Bulletin*, vol. 35:1, Spring 1940, pp. 14-30.

Skinner, Orin E. "Stained Glass Tours: New England." In Stained Glass Association of America. *Bulletin*, vol. 61:4, Winter, 1966/67, pp. 26-49.

Skinner, Orin E. "The Thirty-Second Convention of the Stained Glass Association." In Stained Glass Association of America. *Bulletin*, vol. 35:3, Autumn 1940, pp. 70-84.

"Stained Glass for the Home." In *Arts & Decoration*, vol. 28:4, Feb. 1928, p. 74.

"Stained Glass has a U.S. Renaissance." In *Life*, vol. 6:14, April 3, 1939, pp. 30-32.

"Stained Glass Symposium at Metropolitan Museum." In Stained Glass Association of America. *Bulletin*, vol. 34:2, Autumn 1939, pp. 66-68.

Thomas, Roy Grosvenor. *Stained Glass: Its Origin and Application*. New York: Privately Printed, 1922.

Thomas, Walter H. "The Girard Chapel, Philadelphia." In *The Architectural Record*, June 1933.

Valentine, Uffinton. "American Glass." In *The Architect*, Aug. 1929, pp. 508-510+.

Wheeler, Walter F. "The Casement Window Returns to its Own." In *House Beautiful*, vol. 53, Feb. 1923, pp. 120-121, 164, 167.

Wheeler, Walter. "Possibilities of Leaded Glass." In *House Beautiful,* vol. 52, Sept. 1922, pp. 214-215, 249.

"Wrought Lead Grilles of Decorative Design." In *Arts & Decoration*, vol. 35:3, July 1931, p. 53.

Yale University. *Reports Made to the President and Fellows.* New Haven: Yale University, 1911/12-1924/25.

Yale University. *Yale University Catalogue.* New Haven: Yale University, 1860, 1907/08.

Yale University. Buildings. *Decoration of Sterling Memorial Library.* 2 vols. of facsimile copies (mostly negative photostats) of illustrations used.

Yale University. Library. Clippings pertaining to the Yale Library. Scrapbooks.

Yale University. Library. Pamphlets on the History of the Yale Library.

Manuscript and other non-book materials from the Yale Manuscripts and Archives Collection:

Yale University. Librarians' Records. Sterling Memorial Library - Decoration.

J. G. Rogers Papers.

A. P. Stokes Papers.

Yale Miscellaneous Papers.

Yale Picture File.

Yale University. Treasurer. Building Committee. Records, Minutes, Contracts and Subcontracts.

Yale University. Treasurer. Invoices. On the building of Sterling Memorial Library and all buildings designed by Rogers at Yale.

A stained glass rondel in Medieval style (image based on an early playing card?)
created by G. Owen Bonawit in the 1930s for his own house in Ridgewood, New Jersey.
(Image courtesy of Peggy Bonawit Labash.)

This work was designed and composed in Palatino using QuarkXPress by
Gay Walker. Printed by Everbest Printing Company in China through
Four Colour Imports, Ltd. of Louisville, Kentucky, this title was Smyth-sewn in
a limited edition of 3,000 copies. Photographs are by the author except as noted.